THE POET'S
Assortment

ANNETTE STOVALL

authorHOUSE®

AuthorHouse™
1663 Liberty Drive
Bloomington, IN 47403
www.authorhouse.com
Phone: 833-262-8899

Published by AuthorHouse 07/11/2023

ISBN: 979-8-8230-0711-5 (sc)
ISBN: 979-8-8230-0710-8 (e)

Library of Congress Control Number: 2023907634

Print information available on the last page.

Contents

Heard of One Spring Morning

That morning spring the sunlight more,
Tweet, tweet how beaks happy with sounding.
Whoop-dooo sounds it seeming squirrels had more.
Hooray my first in hooray behind
night after night the measure.
Afterall, why came the pounding back, wet clan
from another landscape amount for whistle
howled the aura in group fan
switching wet to how changes.
This wet goes dry till next it crowds more rain.

Case For The Vision

Success I'm witness to the swoon.
The sterling teapot in brim full
existing not without the counterpoint room
I fashion right approach to lyric multiplies spell.
And free to choose the county town house in season,
I go from winter to where spring for warming the approach.
Here servants few in voicing scored some impressive reason
for how they trample on to pick from blooming so free
five hundred marigolds have nothing else do except
intermix blends beside tree reared blooming more such due
purple jacarandas dancing spring rites ritual evidence
I enjoy the view.
Where dining roses thorn festival spikes my finger tips blue.
Can't you see what this my dreaming all it coming to?
Phrasing prank and pleasure in what I would had if
could had.

Untitled

Slow drips go away and back come
drench signal as if drums into drumming
Employ intruder galoot no blame
if standard fount would narrow drought runs.

Her Voyage Came

She had fine house had a pool.
She had a bit charm grammar
and skill you knew she'd been to school.
She had fidelity spouse and child
what else on consonance thrived.
Her spice lived with her heart quickly pounds
and heart next raps a soft rap.
Devotion jubilation's part in church
if tempo spiced the psalm time she'd clap.
Now had time she having ticket.
"Here comes the voyage she wants in.
A transfer plat waits" they all toned in.

They Were There

Who all was there?
The Lawyer
The Padre
by the Caregiver.
And child none not even husband
around where poorman cousin.
Behind main utterance she none heard
they came where dry thirst and relatives
all 4 around they seated.
Announcement rang from that proof list
just one inherited all she listed.

Youth Remembered

My early days once had youth
had fun with childhood games
abided where my aunt that neighborhood.
Then one day I went had none the happy games.
Where did my youth disappear gone
like where gone how vanished the roof,
vanished the lot and play how vanished the games
I once played, escape chased to memory saved.

Essence To

This essence devotion
of sworn to church pew
till off pursuit there, chase saddled
with chase what service do.
And where shifted hailed the trust
devotion makes the vassal
flavor to another trust.

A Nighttime Dream

I dreamed up there where His throne to however
shaded entity, my regards
what I espied a scene where at hand
a better mark for beauties plastered land,
like do shrub berries, daffodils, birds, trees.
On the other hand
endless poverty hurts and crude ache disease
with even more of ranked mention
street crimes, prejudice still and horror's war.
Some picture could millenium
could best bestow mankind ecstasy amid remorse.
Oh He said he knew much of this.
And glad I'm fame in rank what he could miss.
And past He staked stars, He said down here a man's true
worth
a curse or love for service this earth.

What's the Good Taste in News Today

No rabid storm or hurricane every month.
The coast got clear for people walks come.
Your wash bounced up bright garbs eluded gray dim.
The wet soup steeped in pot steel got mix to bowl rim.
And what some hearts to want fixed got rank to honor pursue
denouncing wife, child and else abuse
to needing stops like rusted kettle flung from much abuse.
The mood changed with some assailed some grievance where
    tossed
to grievance allotment wrenched of a stand for mood repose.
Eyes cried real tears for pal death I stewed over.
But something comes of he was very old when life over.
Some know what due prevailing hunger filled anew.
Would said here leak a start in good news?
I leave subject all said up to you.

Right foods and liquids next for the wait.

Conviction Served

Oh what mischief in the air.
He lost had seat on justice stage.
Official town dicision maker
had his curtness overruled.
Look for else rank he could be schooled
suddenly seemed unfair.
Travel to where no measure curt,
unheard of. He'd felt worse to stun him like
dart carved in struck nerve.
Dare he head for another post?
Then where trek like stranger inquisitive
to unit could stake hapless post?
Came the answer,
On the train a judge in transport.

The Prisoner

He was the prisoner confined
that now the prisoner freed.
Which what schooled man now freed?
Was he much the noble deed
released him out from inside
from once ignoble greed.

White Clouds

Those yet white clouds galore
do none restrain grants moving slow.
Light they motion far yet visible
the marvel of I witness down here
and gape behind the more I'm up close.
So else but white like foam in rotate light
I ride a day on delicate light clouds white
go Oh so dim by night they so invisible.

What Beyond One History

His thinking he was one of who male
did toil with tote that bale
do lift to heavy woodpile.
Something more hard labor his in tobacco
and southern cotton and nut field.
Was all some things he read or heard about
in some author memoir that real?
He was older though yet young enough still
to know what history tells his daydream.
He had better living now
that free to rank what life to mean.
Free speech, some good yields and firm pill
to swallow what past woe be gone to
what free speech wanting relief to woe still.
More he thinks on not just him regrets how life
to who brave now owns what martyr grave.

Visitors for Dinner

Visitors who came to dinner
be male and female gender,
why have you come anyway.
I don't like your strike play.
You in and out the house come
resounding signal in your hum.
Why must your persistance serve
for smack the motive frame mine and nerve.
Don't step in plate frame nor cup near,
words landed on deaf ear.
Grab tree with fruit in the yard
to find won't be hard.
Three fast into my coffee cup they hied.
The verdict all 3 died.
Life's tough round where fruit and house fly.
Why can't I other lodging try.

Untitled

Mrs. Viola living simple
Like the violets margin fleck
the rude grace they so air.
Then dying last like anyone
of wide digit.
Her total grave none sparing.

Man For The Chill

Deck the jacket, guard the suit,
Pick the hat, choose the coat,
Pack inscripted suitcase,
I'll all such need Pioneer man said.
Slam the dish, scrap the tray I made.
Feast there wondrously in array,
Clamp the boot, swop the sheet,
Close the window, shut the blinds to.
I don't know when for the hour exact
But do know my originating fantasy makes
I may like where autumn sacred
if site assembles more chill there.

Untitled

Now man was choral singer,
a darn good one I'm told,
wouldn't you know upon discovery
they located him
wearing lavender chorus robe
with dangled tassel sheer in robe cap
beside him handy on chaise lounge.
Slick oil my shoes they heard him say.
To glory prominence I'm on way.

If You Could Go

If you could go somewhere
you thought no depth that coast,
I doubt you'd ramble where
some fossil finds there most.

There is too with low street
the corner temple post
deep nigh once bassoon beat
it toned for premier coast.

And'ever sea winds blow
it never stone and rock served
discordance in mind heard
that note late you could know.

He Had Fame

He was joy enjoyed the notes he sang.
With joy he stirred his fans ear
where feet happy tap to his lyrics.
Some practiced step to they'd hear
the spirited vocals his rang clear.

His fame was lauded for what it was.
His was lively tunes they half extolled.
For bass notes off spirited
made him one more prophesy on fame
to flagging melody short fame.

Another fame had best rhythm right
it shipped his go from first renown gone
to type he's preacher orator
how switch to an altar zone.
Now his is new life he spirits home.

Royaltʏ Scene

At home he wears how differs robe
he places form in colorful hue.
The flats his how framed with gold.
And robe his choice of purple hue
do more for morn than for devotion
drapes eve in how unfolding fade hue.

On street he wears a varied sleeve
he places arm in sleeves designer hems.
The boots his how reflect glitter.
And cuff is crowned with bluish gems
he dons day or night of dark promoted.
He likes how shawl sky of glimmers in.
Proposal Island where is his throne
this prince for be shipped to wed upon.

Harvest Search

What was I hunting, was it God,
Or blossoms on the universe renewing
Or more freedom, house, yard and love yet blooming etcetera.
Oh, I found turf stars of that before acquiring my knack had last.
Where was I when harvest had it staging turf of that.
The country plot had once gems in fair ground for pick
the heavy sprouted greens, tomato vines starred climbing yard
    stick
where chain fence alight where padded paw hare scurried digging
and marriage breathing still where stalk corn brightly ribbing,
the garned case now none same.
Things I had I don't. Now I'm ageing some things reap no
    care for same.
Was I mop soaking up things turned loss? if add soap to reason.
The Official ad-mix merger system tricks or treats.
When poet I am let off equipping once was birthing of gender,
something else loss I would not resume having.
Some laud who I am for the better. They stall rekindle
what mound is life circling like also windy spring sweeping
    what for
here should net heap than patch we could before an ending
    rate near or far.

Untitled

Turn up the heat some prayed.
So little He bestowing this now Autumn
evaded better latch they would stand
the soothing keyed in to harvest.

Tokens in Recall

The pan, the rolling pin, shine glasses
had etched on design
all tokens of one such time
my living not just I'd recall
assortment for here recall.
Refinement grand now fade on tarnish
I could and won't mind if I do
slick shine the silverware grand.
The ancient age art I'll inspect
for could toss which paintings flawed.
I'll keep a few blue rim dishes fine.
The family once then was mine
excludes some. Two died, some live still.
It's rarely a guest may come
that once had.

Something Missing

I remember once upon a time
delivery was an upgrade fine.
Premiere behind the mate life ceased,
a supply went missing.
A love delivery fast ceased.
Switch now tokens concept.

Here by the Flowers

He stood by here the bounty
arising sends the beauty
to fresh how the blooming yellow and pink rose
how rose set adjoining orchid set shade light.
And not without what birds their clamp do
stripping nectar from amid the flower sets.
Here he would live at a house so near
if mainly just for view and pick a few
from the valley gave amount
to bring safe home to someone blooms anew.

Choice in Fruit

Lemons, oranges, grapefruit,
plus apples, pears, peaches
to added more to the length grows
on choice pick to eat.
Of which their fructose I'm reminded
some with slow arm to pick.
And seldom arm in sweet fruits remind
to many pick the rich desserts instead.

Splendor With Flowers

From home to search where arose
the land adorning every splendor,
she went where orange hue crowning daffodils
close by so yellow buttercup gems unfold.
There she gathered by the hour
flowers of the better grace to share.
And to be there from face down and up the wall
to height she stared in high ceiling,
time and again she would come there to call
so gently something words to declare
Oh Amenity Day!
I have found more grace to share.

Untitled

Those gleaming stars how numberless
they twinkle tremble how alarming.
Traveler if reached should wonder.

I Had A Certain Plant

I had a certain plant for grow
free if cozy
where near my threshold floor.
And limited reach it stunted growth
I wanted more from the flower top bit love satisfied
with cactus arc growing slow.
Then summer adorned the way arc yielded
to then it reaped more love for plant growing
brimming nearby at fair surplus ground.
Half sad I was of way loving disarm the cactus bulge.
Autumn sounding rinse that year
it hurried arch rise tho yet scars needed shove.
And no disrespect to some who never went
for dumb to more and less affection sent.

Yesterday the Birds

Yesterday the birds had twitter
where sounding clear and sweet,
no wonder if soon their plumage retreat
flocking, doubting if chirps in air
pronounced grand how filmy aura.
And only what some nebs next day twitter
what sorrow birds reflecting
how Oh so dimming shroud curtain.
Where shroud in serve to many undeserving
delivery in to smog deserving.

This Laborer

Law man, rich man, beggar man, thief.
His of the insight it dims on thief
since thief sight from pillar to post
he seeks the victum or bank
of which his blame gives notice.
The only thing of times he took
was free sample from where toil
his duty for in town factory.
Can't deny a man that. And toil
he was up for that. Each sunrise dawn
it seemed beaming on him alone
had laborer hands for strain the labor.
And rank he was like prisoner earns
his freedom heads for slaving job term.
Not true his hound in the hunt
for palace treasure richness huge sum.
Climb esteem his wanted ladder rung.
And reach swank billfold he'd main dodge pebble.
Much this hope in earnest about a turn to
he could net more worth than strain he earns.

Served of Some Ages Elderly

The up in age elderly one
be the man and woman
informed me of how the shift say
to 3 maybe 4 scant meals a day
could rate swell for mental prowess.
Others like the late night owl
stay up late for taper turning in early.
Still others none the hurry
for talk what medicines took
since they rather they take a look
into kitchen cabinet stored
they hunt garlic, salt or baking soda
or honey, vinegar or red pepper more
their substitute power of they other times need.
If I turn like to this they give heed
I may even try take the hint.

Untitled

This twisting and turning in my back
like a wheel turning on its axis.
When will some ache cease to exist.

This Account

We live with much our polluted air
stoops amount to folk
their flu amount and virus.
So real how they lean coarse grades to folk count
as evidenced by mask applied yet.
Add to that how afloat dust mite
the lounger floating on air, this yet
account ill favored like more grade amount
ill favored could more disturb us yet.
Like bucket ills many decades ago.
And still rising population
could lead to ills more.
What is world coming to?
I don't burn for catch the flu
I never yet had before.

Unwelcome Shots

The shots rang out so rapid fire
killing teacher plus students
inside their student classrooms.
And others their desire
first shouted in yard play
had last the young man's gross fire.

In another town one man's wrath
killing people few in crowd.
Strickened sad more who survivals
to shots made wound had some down,
some standing on wound ground.
When will the rage become
right hush upon earth
if the kingdom ever comes.

Looks On The Watch And Go

I looked and sat in church my choosing.
And looked in summer I rode or walked where I'd choose.
And something one time or more my cruise
with look through main event in city that park
I looked between artwork made the eye gaze sparkle.
I looked in town some richer thriving around abandoned
poor,
proof I gave rich and who out on block they live poor.
I rode where vineyard richness only crowning what scaling
vine,
that liquid lavender I tasted grapes crushed into wine.
If more better to eat grapes than quaff juice fermented
I can't say tell for better or less the comment.
I looked behind threshold seminary short lure.
And walked the long hillside and small city provided contour
I looked behind constructed erected anthill
ant penitence around seeming sorrow she crying then still.
Because there was no crust of bread her crumb
for take that day to where her brood alone at home.

Question of When

Headache, backache ailment cruel so.
I went where doctor I asked of leaving when.
Will going be today, tonight, tomorrow?
condition makes my sense for know.
He said not yet but in case you do start to go
then - let me know when.

Ranked of Grown Son

Oh, what escape to corner grown son.
And kin did phone and visit with son.
Now regret for lifestyle lacked starving
some venom secret he guarded.
Yesterday they went for hear the phrasing
grossed pale with ranked investigation
after ill struck son dead on bathroom floor.

The Latter Fee

She craved for which conquest dream
she'd have what merit she deserved.
She had it now her scheme
had stunning way the wall plaque served
in print renown indicated.
Then what in spoiled her conquest fame.
The judge arraignment count
for damage done at route,
"Pay the cost or 5 years in drab cell."
She paid the cost
for emptied glee of her in speed well.
Then victory she fled to new height.

What Price Victory

Some have seen the victory
some never had seen.
Decades marked the call
to so many bled to race freedom
that I cannot say to name them all.

The Move He Countered

They moved the couch, bed, china
to air unique refining
what clarifies for sun better shine
gets flood off muddy life brook.
He stirred self in chair they gladly took
he filled by diversive block
some life styles grand else were menacing.
"Just here on earth with deed
my skill qualifies for help who poor"
with phrasing more, "Is deed none enough?
And here a man consent to
"Hell no won't go.
Get me back inside my door."

Untitled

Pain and misery don't forever groan achieving
if brief stay no right to go slow each season.
Though pain and misery if prolong wide stretch
ignite the ache and groan in seek relief.

Solution Wanted

Blue skies dimming on the upper skyline,
Blue lilies rising on hems they display;
And blue jay freed from become acrophobic
sing me the happy warble while I go way
to hillside rose blanks try for the phobia
tilts the joy from sad to say
some homeless, public too in changes motley crew.
This pavement furnishes injury damages
locals given think a crime.
Ails phobic owning from dirt, air, and grime.
Wash Patrol acknowledge and do quick toil.
These walks need wet remedy to sidewalk soil.

Turn Down The Heat

Turn down the heat.
Such too seldom changing now summer.
Though on city block something lovelier,
ageing eye gaze can't always for the glare.
Your fame, You can do anything from up there
if Your will. For Sure, You have the time.

The Mood With Life Changes

We rejoiced with took the sheen in spring allowed.
Plus less heat allowed certain hours.
We relaxed behind receded storm's lightning flash
and thunder clap less take we took.
We kept face if even sorrow causing our drive took
the dive where landed on sad lips.
Type then we musing this take no all of it,
seeing life how changes temperamental classic
like rainbow aligns hue differs on the arch of it.
We hated remainder for what else we took.
It laid our thinking bare to formulate mean streak like cloud
should suddenly shift.
And when it did, the half of what cared about
resolve how partly giving torrid heat limbs less pain.
And venom some fault else in part relief.
Then in evidence we had gain
was half allowed.
A dream was half reaped, a service half gain.
Indicates for times our choosing no choice
than to half the cheer in rejoice.

Another Prisoner

He was the prisoner knew something
of while his internment then
he could solution in what for him.
He settled it for there and then
he had no what exactly since less
of him for lawbreaker sinned more.
He of once heard how lock up more than
tied to sport outside they loved more.
Then what. Back where inside a blank cell
no life to live where he sorrowed be.
What would he lack if library there
his will to fetch a book from.
It should speed some text leaks info
should speed who grown remorseful out from where
a man feels almost alone.
The one in cell with him too wanted out
from stretch in cell comprising too long stretch.
Stay one more year to him tall fee.
More likely read and read what starred upon
the glory crowned him his early key
unlocked the cell to man out now free.

Late Infirmity

To cafe, store, barber shop
art museum, movie anywhere.
He could take self everywhere
a man wanted, needed be there.
He drove a car even before
guide the motorcycle he rode.
He has adorable wife
where child grown left home they reside.
When illness for hospital bed
it stamped him tied to life almost bare.
Why did what happened to him no tease
to pounding his bone disease.
Frail his ill infirmity he now so
can't chance for open even car door.

Yesterday had classic shaped today more rain
tramped the grasslot blueprinted stubs chaste.

Rare Invitation

A stranger where I began to know
came from category to who tripped had
not much for his category.
I was in authentic space medical hall
where talk he starred serene all
anybody staff said no sin
to hear his talk related upscale floor
came behind his trip up 5 floors
for where invited. Invitation rare tip
in sounded like rare party indicated.
So he came swiftly off the elevator
but to like vacancy roof party
no wine, no band, no heed they discerning
he wanted soothing not without such
he wanted most be there.
He might if search there another season.
Though not without there receive the reason.

Hope or Fantasy

We keep hope even if something
supplements, pills, medicine
won't keep to cure they promise
what sounders vocalized in those ads.
Were they touting hope turn fantasy
did hence for keen pitch glad
they advertising more they air.
What such worked for some was boosting nadir
for else were juvenile and age wanes.
After all to said plus done to do
it all hope down to same we do.
Like wait on cure or on exhale to last breath.

He Walks Pavement

He walks pavement day by day
He hunts meal or shelter temporary
if not he residing in tent.
And seems nobody right intent cares.
He once his gallantry brave and bold
attacking where blood bath war bold.
He's not just poor how stripped of stout pay
was month after month wage.
Doesn't anybody care this man
homeless man the veteran.

A Promise to Keep

The couch, car and luxury else due
her tenant home.
She had kept her luxury promise above
vent pledge to fall.
Dare she face another swank city town
had stoop like fall.
Tho different. Somewhere stoops fall's allotment better
stoops warming hard breeze.
Though where the arranging do what unique
to now her oath quite serious wants there.
Could there spilling seasons warmer air
her good could profit from the upgrade makes air
the bouncer tosses howl to winter too less chill.
In town here she can't stand cold.
Some day she must seek and find out,
be she promised,
what there season all about.

Search for the Lot Rising

He searched for the lot rising
on aisle lane in spice and herbs,
soda, liquor, water, wine galore
plus fodder, wheat, grain and else more.
Once fiery eyes and red boots clerk
once worked where he knew
what others knew such the tip nailed
which all hooked on drugs he'd sell.
Now stranded eyes looked behind he yelled
"You Minister, Manager, any sane
am I stop here from floor I missed.
This drive floor elevator
must have taken me floors up
or back down too far."

This Trip To Somewhere

Her will it looks for location.
Northern grand but what for South.
She may will to Western edge best.
Public this guest standing out
gets no surprize in territory fact
Where sun is hot the arc burning cool
on better noons in fact.
And trees blooming well of any season
even tho smog due to appear.
Temptation no fool,
To there for going no doubt.
And aim she deriving said it clear.
Transition here she comes.
There's room for more guests appear.

Where must earth terrains of mark no file
be terrains none sinning?
Enter - a set date - walk in.

Looking for Destination

Weary the will and body run down
his virtue crowned no sparkle crown.
Next looks he for that landing seat
so sweet acknowledgement claimed sweet.
And haste to that emergent.
Then Mister if you look resolve how
ranked far not far where poor group score
they strip to their confinement.
The said of one knew ritual score
to there no skeleton from escaped.
Now here you see the field
the answer given at Potter's Field.

She Was Gifted

She could sing, act, and had her dance
the jig amount grace etiquette
for this they all cast set
for use where she per chance
on stage her qualified advance.

And, Oh, that sequence rank with childhood
in the moment sequence pledged right
for wed her stardom appetite.
Or wedded be she could
to serving else rank could rank good.

She had now mate who wanted her home.
She lags on renown she ranked next
her sequence toil her excess.
Where island coast had zone
from the puzzlement she did come.

Another Gifted Woman

She has talent to the apex peak.
She can her cymbal clap and play keyboard
piano with peak gusto in to chapel.
Impressive apex also with scold
when gifted grace of her as well.

She's ace when family bass mood peaks
sear glory deserving she scraps their hell.
Aft her mom died she stamped kid flare up
the flare more should less it swell.
And she was graceful age eighteen just.

She has also her moods though seldom such
her sad gospel would peak the mood tears
like plainly now for soon takes leave
my patronage to battle war dreary.
Still I believe spouse I am will soon back home.

From Flunk to Where

He had flunked the science test in classroom
and test for play on basketball court.
Retrospect from that fixed gloom
his ailment drama the bad he'd feign at home.
From there if could he'd go where comparison Hades
the lexicon hint of rich dollar mount plus mirth.
None the savage flaming fire sad doom
his preacher's church sermon's bad worth.
He could not know situation format.
Introspection awarded student here what best.
He'd study and should pass next classroom test.

This Music

God could she sing
any place, any coast
day and night songs
to member anyone
man, woman would listen.
Her heap her wish
and grant perspective.
And misery, joy and be grateful
with prayer, chatter too singing
had less for make tune she'd record.
For afterall she is music.

Two For Conduct

He went to work everyday,
Kept clean, brushed teeth twice a day,
Came to church Sabbath end days.
He had his addiction
less honor to some seldom relief
he gave remark in "So what."
He was Mister Right until he slipped up.

She never gave much to chore day,
Slept late, brushed teeth once a day
and entered Rehab helped
She sank her addiction.
Now leak to folks in the neighborhood
give honor they recite,
"She was Miss Wrong who with now more things right."

Seen On The Path

How those uneasy have believed
How slip intruded two on the lane seen.
The male when hard his fall bereaved
Blue incident wrote his hard slip scene.

More strangely next who ran off she'd wed
Destiny had firm grip on dim blue hours.
Along that budded tint crown outspread
She paled beside her go near flowers.

Swiftly the sparrows crossed in flight
No cherubs purple horn blasting pride.
Grateful for I'm alive I pegged grim night
Like slips I moan tho for two full arrived.

Blue incident gloom path's mound
Had set their move toward outter sleep.
It summons us tho for two summons grounded
Had sped the life toward ends we all keep.

Bliss With Hades

The ecstasy, the sport, elation.
Who even went down to Hades
and came back frolic real his rapport
to his accordance even happier sport
he flipped the card, tossed the ball, and sweet on wine
did true he cleared for the alcohol reached throat?
And no evidence of flame, fire or smoke
of which church minister spoke.
One lexicon fixed Hades almost Heaven.
If strong possibility of that,
we may all saints wanting be there.

Utopia When

So glorious this mix in the air.
Blanket sleet in dry form.
Zip rage in taste heat and storm.
Deadpan tornado and crime.
What mix would flavor majesty pray tell?
Occasion to earth would be fine
if to earth Utopia manifest.

Inquiry With Move

The paperman came asked
if wanted her news be renewed.
She said I won't say yes
I'm moving tonight.
The volunteer came asked
if then her volunteer work due.
She said I won't nod yes
I'm moving tonight.
The social worker came asked
of her if concept given gone right.
She said I won't now speak yes
I'm moving tonight.
The nun came. Quota shade she undertook to ask
if yet her go for that night.
She said I can't say what
for argue the site
of yet my go for tonight.

Where Can You Go When You Can't

You liked to church service go hear sermon where choir
singing happy the Hallelujah chorus.
You selected college go choose the trade you like.
And glad you were if at movie, sport etcetera sight.
But comes a time this in repose with where can you go?
Where can you - when you can't score with go?
Clap by church pew, I many times did and praised God.
Attend my fill diverse group especially college
trained my art, and brief some story writ, I've gone there too.
But where can I go when I can't keep go.
Go in to think plus read something only natural.
Watch the tube where sit and sleeping normal action
then occupation tray on empty.
Where can I go if not out for the food scrumptious I ate
it did add ounce to waist if waist on overload.
Why still. Why back in with what more the idleness would
score
There comes a time when someone in repose
can't keep to interesting advantage jilts stay in too long.
Where can one go when can't keep to go.
Tomorrow I may overcome my stay I'm in more.

Repose can be next for shift.

Another Due Reflection

How real did some coming out go.
Emerald green trees were touching ray glow.
Leap grasshopper vaulted more in view.
Pink strawberries escalated hue.
And cast realm for feast on rustic realm
close by a train in speed run late
by Godly cast I yet how rated
God's Spring Promotion.
Still I hasted journey district link
of another cast having link.
School yard, classroom banner,
stone buildings tall in tinted floor tan
to state promoted my birth.
Not yet I go along my link dark realm
one time I've no reflecting more on then.

Ornaments In Evidence

Ring around the rosy
a pocket full of posies.
Though what here gorgeous none hidden in pockets.
Dangling picturesque in sheen on frame doorknob
the bead and silvery trinket chain glob
like golden glow the bauble headed necklace.
Timber mirror legs too frame colored loops hang
where in the bedroom I looked how jewelry glitter
some sort bit grief it minimized less bitter,
if sparkle gems on framework best.
Still at times I fetch what sparkle plainly best
in smaller chest I rummage where for pearls I find.
And other mount the nickles, pennies, and sack dimes hang
like when times I did and still do buy for self
if simple treat or light reward I awarded myself
for how the verse, art, jewels mostly I made
the made fine of my trade
I showed at coast westerly beach I paraded.
Since I never did sell even every type made then,
Pardon me if shine I favor wear my own type gem.

His Fair Concept

Enter in on the morning
the aura flavor better on spring
be simply chill becomes bold.
Take a look the grand survey.
Here the scene assigning spring
with first on planet gold
sound the wind, storm the gate.
Stake the palm tilts the sway
gets tipplers on wine elate.
Who had his concept on planet heaven
latter dreaming on what for the hell.

What Was it Like to be Single

What was it like to be single.
She came to picture show near
and also to art museum.
One such chop house far and near
allowed she'd smoke with sip coffee.
Sometimes her grave crop a few tears
waltzed on coffee nigh he's arranging
her interest not enough for wed
arrangement sham like in her dream.
Then interesting college course stacked
her independence her fame
that swiftly independence stacked game
her flurry to an altar lane.
Still late night her mate's departure swift
and like the winged geese flee
to altar monument far
from cold inserts his tomb more.
A date from now she could ponder
while looks to heaven sweats more sky,
her been married what was it like.

Her Mood Change

Here was envy right. She despised
the house, the pool, the lawn,
medallion ornamental plaque
and mantelpiece trophy some won.
The skill, the glee and silver teapot
like goods the large and small
their goods too dwarfed her undersized glee.
Was it because poor soul had not all
for which she paid hard toil.
She had her pot, her garments, her rooms
she rented on wages wrung tight.
Then suddenly motive changed from doom
to course cinched her scholar trained
for how net on her trade cinched boon.
And how became her sociable dove,
Now she was love.

Ship For The Cause

The galleon, the steamer, the sloop.
So varied vessel the ship group.
Peculiar vessel I won't fix moan
to I can't yet place where the zone.
To orderly motif I can guess
renown to favor tame there yet.
Though some devotees could want keys
unlock the bank, the groove, the breeze
There no intention can be found
than to laze on silt around.
Been troubled here poor years I'm free.
These locals 'round have agreement
ticket I have no need.
Conductor skipper evade this stop.
Maybe on crew ship some day for the cause.

Seasonal Degree

Some for degrees 90 in spring
that for some same as degree 100.
Some others all for temperature amount swing
at 70 for best score.
So true I must admit here score my amount
up to now spring and summer that show.
This western coast heard of I know
for bowing warm and hot the flame score
degrees fair territory temperature.
Plus zero shame in bow convention load
on winter little starves warmth amid the cold.
Degree extent she manifests bare around beach
the slow driven gust with feed freebie tan
when dark skin awarded mine no tan grand.

Concerns the Moon

Ask me of the moon I'll tell you what.
I see it early morn and night
it flashes gleaming aura it gifts
around and too above our height.
And moves how satellite curving move
it circles earth a length from it gives light.
The full curve is mass like half moon
they both lights visible thanks assigned to sun's
reflection on both seen with go and come.
Moon count in 29 days of slightly loomed
the rate to what the moon census tallied sum
30 to 31 days the new moon month.
Astronauts floated such times with circuit route
their steps they smoothly floated with trek there.
Men stepped for tower once intent for near there.
Aliens may tripped from where moon to here
some folk believe like mystery said real.
The moonlike Jupiter, Saturn, Mercury
and planets else glow even on weak gray skies.
Where do I get off where they align.
I cede to list here to end of the line.

Concerning Planets

How going those planets.
Mars the 4th from the sun,
impressive red globe rounding sun heat slow.
Mercury small and closest sending slow
circles in on sun.
Venus the second close bending near
to also rounding flame heat.
And to some Venus winks remembrance charmed
platonic love and love more real the heat sweet.
Jupiter no spread lacks large, Uranus, Saturn
with others like above all named for some God.
Lest jot urge forgets, planet earth slow drive third
in circle 'round the sun lights the advantage
in light to any on planet earth wide breadth.
Planets, what more secrets etcetera.

How Green Their Terrain

How green was their terrain this folk
with green grasses terrain grandiose style
I implicate by way Kentucky grass seed
esteemed so the best. They living though where
bend in the road this far is not far
from where I lived at rock road and overlapped woods near
I had but to look beside then neighbors attractive yard.
I marveled how thicker trees green growing in the rear.
I fumbled at front gate some people knew they
just had to call somehow ahead they go through.
How new green I was to grass floor I small noticed so green
where my living till when moved to that neighborhood scene
latch I espied had silver hued gate latch locked.
Some children climbed the fence like the adored one I love
she brought me fruit from verdure greenish yard bough.
I wondered with keen thinking time to time
who were these people living in the house ranch style.
It was hard thinking these people of the green would think
unkind of me to enter by the green of things.
I'm sure they would have me welcomed if behind the gate
I'd reach their home where what sort they to state,
Welcome in my friend.

Give My Regards

I've searched heaven and also the seasons rich lay
said aught in zero voiced would bury the sway
to even if kins danced to or they said gets triumph wide and
strict.
Worship the One and universal here bank holds nature,
What a hefty dance to pay.
Some say flora cluster and One in same symphony they age.
Consider phrasing some had rhythm sounding stern in
wage us
more than one tip tip "Water all the port."
A huge thirst will crust again palate ceiling.
However is you praise, hold quartz or loathe dance to
minimum wage,
I'm heed to triumph if dwarf menace like some have or will.
Give my regards to here and/or the One.

To the Fair Scene

How fair how season now the scenery
the cute flower pleats here have common
spry limbs in poke the entwining
trees in how curving loops to bills now vocalizing.
And serving fair notice of how spring
the scene in prorating
what now fair outcome this arose.

Rainy Day

Rain, rain goes away
Come again another day.
I have the boots, I have the umbrella
that good for April permitted shower itself,
do rain to dry pavement, mankind, church steeple I once
    prayed below
and tried praying at home not just for rain the one hour a day
    score,
fixed time so many initiated commenced praying.
And may had phrasing segment ran then even for how the rain
could long wash sidewalk grubbiness cleaner begets dirt and
    grime again.
Now drops eluding do more the same.
Alright go! Your liberty allowing drying out sometimes.
I've noticed before you leaving how arranging emission pounded
large and short your measure ran.
As witnessed how umbrella drips wet missile still few yet pound.
Though other times over few enlarging shower emission.
Some having wish like here I phrase
Don't swiftly switch criterion departed we miss.

Untitled

Spring day sun shining thru the rain
there is no forever drench watered storm.
And not unlike cloud the drubber in some
cannot at forever unexposed.
Storm fetching light it arms the attack.
And shining light it bled and humbled cloud
before it made drubbing more reaped
if not some bit of misery forsook cloud.

Youth Talking

Your lady meant for honor
you honor me. Your much presence so wills me,
If you game for I'm arranging my skill
for talk here of some things.
You should not need the overmuch medicine spills
more pills to bloodstream.
Vaccines too work attacking 'specially flu or virus
if in home you walk or your switching seen outside.
Alarming service text to folk it broadcast
"Delay wash day, stall the vacuum."
Best to pop the ache on soothing couch may do,
so said the man in youth.
I woke to flame ignited premature heat flash
that spring in bloom I gazed by a window sash.

Beautiful Flowers

Beautiful flowers
high top lilies, red rose, trench begonias,
aster, daffodils, pink geraniums
white carnations etcetera.
what to arranging bloom flaps arise real
Like poppies orange crowd arrange
for state one I live.
Blooms they differ flap rise they color
main for pick or buy unless you order.

To Spring Conversion

Come howl wind for stay a while with spring.
Shiver the cast inserted scorch in the air
won't stay the breeze to tree and hedge.
And whatever else performance you stay
do not for the stay
dodge draft nor cool the rooms too cold.
Then we can all have little dismay
about how the blow inserted in diverse way
residing still with swing to the cold.

A Change Reaped

Threaten, stalk, hiss. Real the dishonor
the boy and girl bully wedded.
Till hiss made soon to wither,
and threat and stalk made to instead
surrender dishonor bare soon as wedded
their scripted verse of not far Temple school.
Then they made dead to shame I incurred
like I was dead to their scorn foolery.

Spotlight on This Juvenile

He has his worthy sight drawn
to he assuming this could be his worth
in fixing things like the chair seat worn.
He could yet assume he sends youth something worth
when he trips bias how runs nullified
if his correction shipping bias from how friend.
He briefs the anger more he dwindles threat
to spunk worth elusive of him back 'round fret.
To Court, Probe like who Skeptic
my sideburns cured, and tip wants the feedback sage,
Can't you see I can be redeemed
his juvenile tip in this age.

Much Toil In Question

She certainly did have impressive article collection.
Dressed up dolls, tinted glassware glamorized sketch,
Chic brooch she made and glitter beaming idleness perfection
congealed in varied shades her jellylike gel candles.
Where might it just lead this now so much capability she
    stands.
Would finding rare notable items and making class
    particulars
build up next for she'd possess
entrapment tangled reward begot from straining forward
    toward
something awarded her more wide excess?
I used to be sacrificed exorbitant mass to I'd pursue.
So I'm no service hastilly engineers revealing what best she
    could do.
What service would I be anyway to whom created or collected
    else
for her womanhood craving else
gift cards, jewelry, stoneware artifact antiques else she saved.
Suddenly gumption shenanigan here selected "Come assist my
    sewing
It's only few hard stitches more to go."
I answered said no, having no intuition I would, given time in
    passing
offered less for try few could turn more I'd assist.
When should overdoers learn seek more peace away from
    certain time
overdone on hard chore they assist.
The local guardian indicated specifically aiming today
time I'm in relaxing I maybe then I would pray.

My Confusion Shelfs

Confusion on cabinet shelfs
      headache pills
      pressure pills
      depression pills
      eye strain drops
      hip, backache pills
      fish oil caps
      supplement pills etcetera
the long line for the cure.
Sometimes I ask myself if I should
have to need all these. Fast I threw out
some old for new confusion growing stout
again mob pill I moan the swell.
Will I never be well.

Pain will be.

What's It All About

What's it all about human?
We work, sweat, slave the hard toil somewhere
when some others work the home agenda somewhere.
Some days I'm no sweat ruminates at home I'm dull to none
than I sit, sleep, eat, rest till day dawning on sun.
I must confess I've scored at times with rest counts. And
    count I could be after
how dawning on less burns bright especially on find fad or
    craft.
I once my rest reposed prolonging length scored my get up
    and go
slow the momentum moves had frame mine looking obese
    though.
Drink plenty water some comment yet, but how much gets
    plenty enough.
Meanwhile, many feign sleep won't sleep when home and
    such
the job duty, college funds lost to sad hurdle dawning on
    recession
and high inflation cost go up and down.
Like how also do race relations up and down.
Work, rest, rise, chill out, heat up, arouse brain cells their
    work.
Is it all about keeping our inner clock working?
What's it all about human?

Don't Kick Me When I'm Down

Don't kick me when I'm down.
I've raised 4 kids, kept house, done diverse jobs.
Attended husband on way out.
Everybody won't suddenly deserting broad daylight
no quick notice in where and when.
Where will we begin for sure a transit will begin.
Will I be then where friend or kinfolk they should care
how member this down at city property the house somewhere.
Where will we if employee some careful though careless.
The stain is at some inappropriate nursing homes.
Missis Jones her months long stay roomed where kin roamed.
And flawed strength hers did even there had bitter gripe moan.
The years my mother in one distant hospital
her last behind walls had times my beef to air on treatment.
Gets sad to say it happens as I grimace the frown.
People do get mistreated when down.
Please, don't kick me when I'm down.

He Came Back

He came back to wife like he said
from where he had the priviledge
right of his escape bank.
He'd heard how glorious cast on ledge
had cast on paradise of such
rare orchids, birds, plush tree blush.

Soon idle who encampment son
went blank to sparkle bush and peacock.
Instead he found advantage won
advantage he'd sleep like a rock.
Ask here a minister ghost like me,
to wife he said,
his message same like mine.

Untitled

Heart beating fast with breathing slow
and cough undefeated.
Was this fate's last alarm?
No Doctor, no Priest,
no Count, no Magistrate,
no anyone having been clued
of the misery like unto her
would covet what the implication.

Her Rationale

Oh this pounding much the rain!
It ever strands thunder with lightning.
And how the drench at now all week
how spring of some persuasion
puts chills in the air.
And here the tenant rent not fair
where port none the same class port.
Who not for the residence here
is making ready arrangement for coast
the bright life dims on forever lonely,
her in honest judgement.
Hail the taxi.
This maiden now ready,
Destination home.

Liquid Death

I was directing my way on foot
when I gazed alarming sign
the taped on Liquid Death
had inked on cans this truck design.
Would liquid bring on death?
I phrase in true for namely some
swamped on alcohol unlike some
would try chasing swamp alcohol dry.

My Poet Recall

"Come up to the podium gain award" of speech broadcasts
"Outstanding rhymes could no many poets master."
It swings recall to dimming recollection still
of once I lived where corn and crop greens great deal.
Since of another town my church Poet Laureate queen
appointed me where I began delivery of comes out
to pew member poem lingers verse till forgot.
Yet this brain matter still spinning my verse acclaim
expressed where audience mine none same.
"Do not let doom on parade dismantle glory
from every chapter writing on your story."
And so forth. Another verse start began acknowledged
"Everything we did was fun."
No, I won't go next changing euphemism here I charm.
Some rhymers metaphor in trees to wave arms.
Of course wee short fun wedge could even reach tall fun ledge.
"Come to podium own the prize" the strangeness said.
Even with these poky legs I might believe it one day.

This One Summer Day

Warm air was breathing air in this one summer day
was yet how hot enough at eve
it charred my skin to mimic baked tree branch.
And timid little drips from humid twig leaves
made firm strands my hair to look wee damp.
I was not just one paused in walking quick step
the curb this eve when friend along too.
Her selected sentence volunteered offered what kept
my ears peeled to minuscule voiced in say
of added up to ice cream the most she had,
her joy on short tripped vacation.
Afterwards with back she was this happy glad
for back with home she losing 10 pound weight she gained.
She had secret about how, my hedging on I'd pry.
Suddenly surprised me secret she had
she vented in said hers was a cabbage diet.
My age old grandmother her secrets too had.
South state she from did voice for more freedom there ring?
How old was she prithee tell?
What other meals could she like other than meals boiled?
Cinch is the friend nor she never started with
I search it not said, "Drink I drink often water."

Time Moves On

Time moves on as move should
and hangs with deed counts
the score with pad years.
Even if grant hand counts the few more.
A grant off apt assigns years.
Especially for who dining resolve
before deed a latter term done
with hard on upgrade commission.

Untitled

As we grow we spot
lilies and mold
fungus and printed fluff glow,
seen classics on earth
do how retraining stems.
Tho some carve blotch like age
we own can't escape.

Another Spring Day

Another morning sunrise springboard
to afternoon sparrows caroling
another tenor near upon day goes
for day star surrenders rose
to rungs on rose still eve I'm gone.
I'm sometimes not at home
to dims on plat of mine illusion
some day my so sure admission.

If butterflies a driving force like bees equipped
And bees were slow diving like the sated butterfly,
How less bother defining difference.

One Sorely Met Day

I once with city town my trip way
I vacationed I was close to near
of town I live tho scald heat there unlike day
I half remember episode that event.
The cast rays how flashed the route and public
scald the heat, scald the route
in town where sagebrush and palm tree stout
raised no say to how fast I ran
for pause below awning scald town lacked glare for
the cooler fever shade I ran for.
What good if scald in gigantic spring turned bleak
to chill stayed. And quest to Nirvana partly warm,
I'm not of there to request,
What good especial if drift there shifted best
from scald to chill to warmer shawl air just.
Decision making ranks decor none such
to first how switching spring aura that much.
The other if change switched to how if should
spring stay the heat, it won't outlast cedar wood.

Regards to Husband

When my husband dying in the hospital
June 5th of years ago and too soon,
I found his youthful going in quick haste
with what arranging
slower say in worded say
until he nearly unconscious.
His much the kind his love I'll long miss
where other joymaking love we shared.
Now memory remnants kiss
the moments come and go my flash back scene
with other love interest we once shared
like aired on the picture show screen.

Meditate on Themes

Meditate on themes a few anytime.
Even if after bold sun returns light.
Or when stars aglow gently shine
when eaves and city lights blurry shine.

Think of day comes with light who some
like dole to poor county member nourishment.
You reasoned glad this none your task sum.
Others have arms firm with get job done.

Ruminate on shaking hands grand
where the superb professor or savant
thaws your sense to more you understand.
Things I penned in journal mine spread out.

When was there never even a reason
to not search journal, tabloid or season
when a person would lack things even
for meditate on 'specially if a poet.

Her Mood Then

Drapes the rose to eyesight dim.
Sings the bird to hearing slow.
So was her mood with gloom elevated.
Small wonder she evaded knowing
else for the gloom way scene.
Someplace the stalk and lea solace
none rare if better ease staked there.
Nowhere she staking assuredly solace
for hers the less more solace.
Swift guide put joy and scramble around notice
to spring her hour is yet and where the realm
to stranding winds put bliss and memory.

The Spirit Back

He was the type his glad smiling face
with limit wrath to less demoralized the irate storm
that went missing to my severed heart his love placed.
Sad his missing went like the love we shared
half gone with how the plus he gave 'most every week.
So unexpected my sad glee would switch pale flare up
contention I'm sending fuss his to joys he almost speaks
this back to where spirit soul refreshens.
Reserved moments as if unfold from more stiff grave enfolds.
His right for be here sends the mate surrendered back
in spirit only just for long or not long necessary his encore
performance to memory not all gone from what years ago.

Oh My, those were the years!
One grinning from ear to ear.
Another one to modeling short jacket.
And one or two for sly with designing
the only one or two pranks.
Those 4 children young loves of mine
I'll never own again
while still I live on earth remain.

This Air

Dust in the air
Smoke in the air
Auto fumes in the air
All constituents of smog.
When will ozone, trees, meadows
the air wholly sweep.
Will tomorrow's population visible?

If no claim for grab the phone lot in pitch sent
or I don't some days reframe gaze to flowers,
you know on bed or couch, contentment
mine in sleep like dead to the world's hours.

Untitled

Friends, kindred this human
for sure will go away.
If and when again I return
I should be the same or changed
a better human.

Search for Pot of Gold

Taxi, taxi
unlock the door
I'm going there.
Taxi driver he said
it's no secret
many, many want I know where.
Tell me where end of rainbow
I'm heading there she said.
And much for I'm due my due pot of gold.

Laurels to Gentlewoman

Where has Miss Gentlewoman gone
from gentleness to shine her smile.
Her social service official
on justice she of a long while.
And sound church commission less a chore
to hers no lack where temple row
since pride in teaching Sunday School.
In practice less the frown she'd show.
Be sad, weep, be happier some
for exempted from crowded earth crush
her go to Eden glorious
some prophesy assuring such.
Though some yet voice in don't know
since never even been there before.

Untitled

Oh how today this cloud renown.
And gust blowing film inside nose
on local sense yet sane
if shudder entered where it reposed.
Pattern strong day on spring unique
just makes awareness, "Oh how the heat."

Me One

The teacher lesson to class came through.
The prominent orator to raise words
his best must do.
Trade owner sweat he did trade done.
The mark I start on do commission grand
I first look to me one.

This Drill Amount

Meditate, read with mend the phrase
day and night
the pack this group amount especially
for poet action or who writer.

Untitled

Professson dines penmark
nets the drill
shapes talent.

His Paradise Town

How real his gaze on local paradise
Social singing of the birds
a soft melody sings. Plus the blue skies
to rapid pounding of the rain
when rhythm let free.
And pavement more in paved nice.
He was happy where this new in base town
he walked to witness summer
bright the rose and bright iris nicely crowned.
And how this new around Paradise essential town,
his also sight on local Paradise there times
a real gray dinginess cast looms at times.
Still his was genuine attachment real for where live.
He had his abode and else key yields.
Still his a thirst for might find best his base town dessert
less gray the atmosphere remaking best worth.
Let's face it. He is his traveler stranger
His fame in stalking Paradise town yields he'd gain.

Untitled

Shade lilies were still tint beautiful
on the field yet rising Blue Monday.
Shade in accorded still thorn, it wrings form
to shedding rent dries out,
If partway like September would own.

Her Confession

It was in her namely core heart
how scene this outside scene
had outstanding tall how steeple
on the vacant lot temple scene.
How could that be even
For her in earnesty confession.
Many sermons I've witnessed heard
and perception how chorale I've praised.
She also that ideal time
conception piety she raised.
She knows too by grace be saved.
Now door I'm knocking knock knock
my plea, tell why the lock.
Whatever sufficient my award
it's how rewarded I'll net
if even sometime I did wrong.
Still her in earnesty core heart said.
Turn around it's not your time yet
came the answer back said.

Was It There

Was it there all the time
The whole knowledge of the rhyme.
The wind was blowing storms we felt
When marigold wavered right and left.

Forecasting more took a stalwart stand
When folk vigil grand and not grand.
We cared less for scaling high mount
And wished for none snow on fall's fresh count.

The land gave qualified hint.
But did it say all it meant
That was yesterday's gain and sorrow
Coming on the coattails of tomorrow.

It Comes Again

Another year another reason
the hedges yet standing,
the spineweed yet,
the tree fringes yet in on
still squirrels climbing
still birds rounding.
Up to now no unit skipped rising
till now autumn
exhausted skirts in flower strains
the first in strain sleeping.

Comes with press for top rung a feasible shift
up or down.

Printed in the United States
by Baker & Taylor Publisher Services